Tanks going into battle with the Infantry on the 25th September 1916.

Preface

The First World War is a forgotten war for many of us, almost now lost from first hand memories, yet it had an effect like no conflict before it. Many thousands of Cheshire men were called to arms, for a cause that was to shape our country and mould a new era. It revealed many things, but not least of all exposed the gallantry of men like Pte. Thomas Alfred Jones of Runcorn.

His courage, endurance and heroism during the First World War was to distinguish this quiet, solemn man, as the most decorated infantryman in the annals of the 22nd (Cheshire) regiment. 'Todger' Jones, as he was always best known, still provides one of only two Victoria Crosses ever awarded to serving infantrymen in the Cheshires.

Todger's remarkable, single-minded feat on the battlefield of Morval was heralded as one of the most daring acts of the First World War, yet there was more to his life and adventures than could be portrayed through this one event. This book intends to provide an impression of Todger Jones' experiences of war and at the same time, expose something of the unparalleled ferocity of Flanders and the Somme.

Dave Thompson

On the blood-stained fields of Belgium,
'Midst the thunder of the guns,
Runcorn lads are bravely trying
To break the spirit of the Huns.
Great accounts they have to settle
With the Kaiser's grey-clad ghouls;
When Cheshire men are on their mettle
The Hun will find they are no fools.
"Second to none" – that is their motto;
The Fighting Fifth, their well-earned name
We are out to teach the Germans "What ho,"
To win for Cheshire a lasting fame.
Thro' Belgium mud they march to battle,
The trenches against the foe to hold;
'Midst cannons' roar and muskets' rattle
Cheshire lads are ever bold.
Side by side they've fought together;
Seen brave comrades bleed and fall;
Side by side they'll fight for ever
And give the Germans pills of gall.
Underneath the red clay some lie;
Life sacrificed, but duty nobly done;
Heaven bless the men who fight and die
For King and Country and Home.
May the corn in gallant Belgium
Draw nutriment from every bone;
Nourish her sons with the gallantry
Shown by those who have crossed the foam
When the "boys" return to dear old England
Victorious and battle won,
Meet them and shake them by the hand;
Say "Runcorn boys, well done."
For they have nobly done their duty
In the greatest of all wars;
Stood unflinching 'fore the Kaiser
For their Country's noble cause.

by Sergeant Bellis of the Cheshire Regiment.

This book is dedicated to the memory
of the four hundred Runcorn men
who never returned from the Great War
1914-1918

A Runcorn Childhood

Thomas Alfred Jones was born at 39 Princess Street in Runcorn, Cheshire on Christmas Day 1880, the festive surprise being the sixth born child of Edward and Elizabeth Jones (nee Lawson). The boy's father was a labourer at the town's Hazelhurst soap works, where he was eventually to serve unflinchingly for 62 years, save for a couple of days sickness. Edward was for 20 years a preacher at the Ellesmere Street Free Church in Runcorn and a well-known worker in the Oddfellow &

The parents of Thomas Alfred Jones.

The façade of the Runcorn National School where Todger was educated in the 1880s and early 1890s. The school building was demolished in 1976 and rebuilt close to the same site.

Friendly Society. The Jones family were of Welsh descent. Edward's father, also named Edward Jones, had been a Flintshire lead miner who settled at Runcorn during the 1830s. Like so many Welsh miners of that time he had been brought to the area by the employment opportunities available at the town's burgeoning chemical works.

The boy who was to become Cheshire's most celebrated war hero was a pupil of the old Runcorn National School at Church Street, as it was known at that time. He entered the austere Church School in 1885

A rare view of Princess Street in Runcorn. The Jones family home is just out of view on the right.

and steadily made his way through the various standards without any particular prominence. Thomas left school in 1894 and served his time as an apprentice fitter at the Hazelhurst soap works, before leaving to become a fitter at the Salt Union's works in Weston Point. Away from work the young man became a well-known member of the Liberal Club, where he won prizes in billiard handicaps, and acted for some time as Hon Secretary of the Runcorn Reserves Football Club. His nickname 'Todger' by which he was best known, stemmed from his childhood passion for football. The small boy from Princess Street became well known for his artful skill in dribbling a football, so much so that other children referred to him as *'Dodger'*, and given that his first name was Tom this evolved over time to *'Todger.'* The name stuck and few people thereafter ever referred to him as anything other than Todger.

Crack shot

In later years the *Runcorn Weekly News* was to write on Todger's early life at Runcorn. They described, *"He has always been popular among his workmates and companions, and taken an active part in athletics of every description. From an early age he had a passion for soldiering, which led him early in life to enlist in the volunteers and later in the territorials. He has always won eulogies from his officers for his smartness, and especially for his marksmanship, having carried off several* first class prizes, often in competition with older and more experienced men." Todger's passion for soldiering began in 1900 when he enlisted with the Runcorn Volunteer battalion and within a short space of time he headed their prize list drawn up by Sergeant Inspector Player. The Runcorn volunteer battalion had been formed in December 1859 and during the Boer War sent three drafts to fight in South Africa but could easily have sent thirty. The volunteers practised at target ranges at Runcorn Hill and on the nearby Heath where the crack shot from Princess Street soon *'distinguished himself by becoming one of, if not the very best shot in the battalion.'* He even received the Territorial Efficiency Medal for his sharp-shooting abilities. Jones spent eight years in the volunteers, and four in the terriers and following on from his 12 years of local service, became for a short spell a member of the National Reserve when it was formed in 1913. In all about one hundred and fifty Runcorn men gave their names to join the National Reserve.

At the outbreak of the war when volunteers were called for at the front Todger is reputed to have been the fourth man to give his name. He sought to join the Royal Engineers, owing to his trade at the Salt Union works but, as a reservist, was ordered to wait until posted to a unit of the army. Very soon afterwards he was drafted into the 1st Battalion of the 22nd (Cheshire) Regiment and, after initial training in Birkenhead, and the military encampment at Codford, Wiltshire, was posted to France on the 19th January 1915. Todger's battalion was part of the 15th Infantry Brigade that belonged to the 5th division of the army.

This postcard of recruits at Codford, Wiltshire in 1914 shows the rookie soldiers acting out the mock execution of the Kaiser. The caption underneath reads, 'What the stiff kids at Codford intend to do to the Kaiser'. Todger Jones is standing on the far left of the picture. A short time later in January 1915 he would be posted to the continent.

5

For God and Country

"He became a first class sniper, first class bomber and guide to his battalion".

**Description of Todger Jones
in the Chester Chronicle (1916)**

The First World War had been set in motion in 1914 by the assassination in Sarajevo of the heir to the Austrian throne by Serbian nationalists and within weeks Britain had declared war on Germany. Thereafter, new recruits began joining up for the armed services at a rate of 33,000 men a day. The horrors of trench warfare, where two opposing lines would become embedded in a situation were neither one nor the other barely advanced was a situation in which Todger would certainly have excelled. His skills as a marksman would prove of great service in this type of warfare, and not surprisingly, by Todger's own admission he was as a consequence utilised within his battalion as a sniper and bomb thrower.

Todger's hometown responded admirably to the war effort. Free access to all public places of entertainment was thrown open to uniformed servicemen on leave, and following a request from the *National Committee for Relief in Belgium* the townsfolk began a frenzy of saving for the war effort. All schools participated in a French Flag Day for what was hoped might be a speedy war. The first sick and wounded soldiers began arriving at the town's Cottage Hospital in November 1914 and with them came the first terrible stories of suffering on the front. They had endured such horror that one soldier decided to commit suicide at the hospital rather than return to face likely death in the trenches. Canon Howard Perrin established a Voluntary Hospital at his Vicarage in Highlands Road, utilising temporary wooden wards in the vicarage grounds. He also bought a motor ambulance to transport soldiers, mostly between Runcorn and Fazakerley. The driver was Rev. Allen, the curate in charge of Weston.

Astonishingly in the years ahead 3,460 wounded servicemen were to be treated at Runcorn.

For children the regularities of school life were placed on hold whilst war raged on the continent, many of the children's fathers were serving in the trenches of Flanders, and their mothers worked in the tanneries and chemical works helping to keep the wheels of industry turning. Mr Lindsay, Headmaster of the Parish Church Boys' School in Runcorn wrote to all scholars in July 1915, *"We usually arrange our annual educational excursion, and many*

Todger and other fresh recruits to the Cheshire Regiment in 1915. Jones is third from right.

of the eldest scholars have been preparing since Christmas to take part in what should have been our fourteenth trip. Owing to the war, there are no cheap rates on the railway, and further, food is dearer, so that as the cost would be so much more, I have decided not to hold it. I very much regret that this course has had to be taken but I feel sure, boys, you will not be more disappointed than I am." Todger Jones' former teacher continued on a sombre note, *"My dear boys, a very dark cloud overhangs our country and the continent. This dreadful war has been forced upon us and our allies by the might of a nation, and if we had not thought it right to keep our promise and protect the weak against the strong, our honour would have been gone forever. Many boys have been helping to collect the names of those who have passed through this school and are serving in His Majesty's Forces. I am anxious that when the war is over and our 'roll of honour' appears, not one name of an old boy who has so readily responded to his country's call shall be omitted. Already, we have a long list consisting of two teachers – Messrs Newport and Youd – and some two hundred and fifty old boys. Quite a number of them have looked in at school when on leave, and right glad have we been to see them."*

It is about this time that Todger Jones writes home giving an account of the death of a fellow member of the 1st Cheshire, Sergeant Albert Darbyshire of Byron Street, Runcorn. He wrote *"We have been out of the trenches again and we have been very lucky, although we have lost about 12 men. Albert Darbyshire's son was killed, he was a Sergeant and was getting back over the parapet after we had finished cutting the wire ready to charge. It did not come off owing to the French advance on our left. We thought the huns would have to retire. We had very bad weather this time, it rained nearly all the time and two nights there was a fairly keen frost. I had a very lucky do the other day, a sausage dropped about a yard from the listening post I was on, but it did not burst."* Todger escaped death and survived what would become the first in a series of astonishing near misses. Not all men were quite so lucky and the columns of the local press were regularly occupied with news of Runcorn and Widnes men being killed on the front. During the first year of the war, seventy Widnes men were killed and twenty-one servicemen from Runcorn, including a Runcorn engineer who was drowned when the *Lusitania* was torpedoed in May 1915.

In Flanders Fields

Todger's battalion, the 1st Cheshires, was posted to Flanders early in 1915. One of his earliest confrontations as an infantryman was at Hill 60, an area that was to earn considerable notoriety during the war. It was a relatively small summit, two and a half miles south east of Ypres but had a real tactical importance. Hill 60 afforded a view over British lines and it was a good vantage point from where movements could be observed. Todgers battalion had been present on the 17th April 1915 when six huge mines, each using a ton of explosives, were used in the initial assault of Hill 60. Todger sent home to his parents one of the most important souvenirs of Hill 60 and the gallant charge the Cheshires led when they took place in the seizure of the hill after the mined explosions. *The Runcorn Weekly News* provided details of his daring in January 1916, *"A union jack was used as the signal to the troops, and the moment it fell was the moment for the charge. The Cheshires were among the first in the charge and in passing the flag, Private T Jones seized it and carried it with him until he came home on leave just prior to Christmas. The flag is a medium sized union jack, about 4ft long, and its association with the charge renders it very valuable to the possessors, who prize it very highly."*

Later in life Todger was to describe Hill 60 as providing him with one of the sternest and most dangerous experiences of his life. In his interview with A.E.Littler he recounted, *"We also went through the battle of St.Eloi, which lasted three weeks (in March 1915). We were at Hill 60 when it was blown up, and we remained in the trenches for twenty days, and after just one night put in another forty-three days, which constitutes a record either in the French or British Army for continual fire-trench work. We were even reduced to the necessity of sewing sandbags together to serve as a change of linen. When the* hill went up it was a sight one can never forget, while the shelling of Ypres was more like a mighty firework display than anything else." Great heroism was displayed at Hill 60. Sergeant Thomas Hallwood a neighbour of Todger's from Princess Street, Runcorn, and serving with the 5th South Lancs Regiment, was amongst those who distinguished themselves in the attack and won the Distinguished Conduct Medal for his bravery in the capture of the hill. Sergeant Hallwood was later killed in another offensive.

Gas

The Germans fought ferociously at Hill 60 and in a desperate struggle deployed the use of gas in their counter attacks. This was their first use of chlorine gas and use of gas shells in any sizeable quantities and it would hardly have been sufficient that the gas marks worn by the British troops were nothing more than pieces of wadding held over the mouth with elastic. Todger continued in his interview with Littler, "I had my first experience, second-hand, fortunately – of the German poison – gas. We had only been relieved the night before, and wanted a rest badly, but at ten o'clock in the morning we received word that something had happened at Hill 60, and it was up to us to try to set it right. We got through Ypres town to the railway cutting, and there came under heavy shellfire. Bad wasn't the word for it, for they were bowling the lads over right and left, and as we got closer their machine gun fire was mowing us down something cruel. Eventually we took cover in the railway cutting and met the Germans coming along four deep. We received orders to charge, and cleared them off the railway line, and then we had to start with the trenches. No sooner had Colonel Scott given the word, as he stood by my side, then he dropped mortally wounded. We didn't wait for further orders, for we saw red, and cleared the second line of trenches. Then we made another charge, and took the original trench, which had been held by the Dorsets. There they sat staring at us. 'Matey, you're relieved' we said to one, but there was no answer. 'There's some hot tea waiting for you in Ypres' we said to another. No answer. They were dead – gassed, and we didn't know then of the diabolical device that had killed them. I was one of forty-three that went out that night to bomb the Germans, expecting that another regiment would take over the trenches from which we had driven the enemy."

Lieut.Colonel A.de Courcy Scott was killed whilst alongside Todger Jones at the battle for Hill 60 near Ypres. The distinguished commander from the 2nd battalion had been placed in temporary command of the 1st battalion of the Cheshire regiment.

The 1st battalion had successfully cleared Larch Wood at Hill 60, secured trenches in the wood and, in the first of several suggestions, Todger missed out on honours. He continues, "We used up all of our bombs, and the Germans began to bomb us in turn. Our lieutenant was the only man with a revolver, and he used it until he had no more ammunition left and was shot. All except three of us and a corporal were either killed or wounded, and the corporal asked me if I could lead them back. I did it, and reported to the company officer, who said he had received reports on which he was going to recommend me for honours. A brave officer – reported from that very day as missing, as was the lieutenant." The death of so many members of the battalion had been a severe blow and a bloody and terrifying ordeal but was to stand him in good stead for what was to follow. Afterwards, Todger's battalion was stood down, only to be shortly mobilised for the impending confrontation in the Somme.

Sacrifice of the Somme

Blow out, your bugles, over the rich dead!
There's none of these so lonely and poor of old,
But, dying, has made us rarer gifts than gold.

Rupert Brooke (1887-1916)

It is hard to quantify the horror that ensued in the Battle of the Somme. The four month conflict was opened on the 1st July 1916 by a completely voluntary army, over half of which was new to battle and had, barely 18 months earlier, answered Kitchener's call to arms. On that first ill-fated morning 100,000 British troops climbed out of their trenches and advanced in a single column, spaced at arms length, which would stretch for more than 14 miles. In the hours ahead more than 58,000 soldiers were killed, making this the worst single day in the history of the British Army. Almost a third still lie under the battlefield, their last resting places unmarked.

Even greater horror than that thus far experienced in Flanders was to face those remaining on the front over the months ahead. The drudgery of days or weeks confined to bitter trench fighting, under heavy shellfire, easily exhausted troops, especially given the capricious weather conditions. Almost every advance above ground was met with machine guns raking the ground, making the mud-filled Somme a living hell. Whenever time allowed, Todger sent regular letters home from the Somme trenches to his parents in Runcorn. In one he wrote, *"Our country needs to think well of the men who have undergone the terrible ordeals and privations, undergone daily by our troops and for my part I am glad to think that those in the homeland cannot realise in the least what the Somme battlefield is like. I hope with you that the hordes against us will soon be crushed, and that we may enjoy the peace of home life again. I am sure it will all be a cleaner and more generous race that will spring than those who have tried to rule with mailed fists, and that the world will forever stop any attempt by any nation to prepare armed hordes to the extent our enemy has done."* It is known that Todger had several narrow escapes during his long period of active service. In one incident he had been struck on his boot heel by a bullet but escaped only with a slight injury to the foot. On several occasions when officers around him had been killed Private Jones had taken charge of the company and as the *Runcorn Weekly News* later records, *"Acted as a guide from the trenches. He has seen an altogether unusual amount of fighting, the engagements he has taken part in including Hill 60, Guillemont and Delville Wood."*

Delville Wood became one of the best known offensives on the western front. Its capture was important because it opened up the way for the taking of Longueval. Before the war it had been a tract of woodland nearly half a mile square. It was covered by a system of rides named by the Tommies after famous London streets and was criss-crossed by trenches named, quite refreshingly, with beer in mind. There was vat, hop, stout, bitter and beer trench but they had a less than sobering effect when the battle raged in July and August 1916. Even when the allies had the upper hand the Germans counter attacked with lachrymatory and asphyxiating gas shells. The South African infantry, in particular, demonstrated immense courage at Delville Wood in the face of such ghostly surroundings. Still, Todger's battalion was saved this misery as they concentrated on the German lines between Delville Wood and High Wood. Vivid impressions of the scene are retold in Colonel Crookenden's book. *"The noise of a thousand distant guns rolled and swelled like the breakers on a rocky shore. While heavy projectiles over-head rumbled to their distant objectives, and high velocity guns spat at the trenches in front."* Away from the wood, the only dug out available for a regimental aid post was in full view of the Germans, on a well-defined road leading to Delville Wood. Stretcher-bearers were easily killed and as a consequence casualties lay in the firing line.

Mined trenches

From time to time descriptive letters from Todger Jones made their way into the columns of the *Runcorn Weekly News*. He had what the paper described as *'the knack of writing some very interesting letters concerning events at the front.'* These appeared even before the events that were to secure his reputation for gallantry. In one he wrote, *"We have had a very rough time again in the trenches. One time it was as if hell had broken loose, shells dropping in, trench mortars blowing the bags down, rapid fire from the German trenches, and to top the lot they had mined the trench and tried to blow it up, but they had gone too deep, and only one or two of our lads were buried, and were safely dug out again."* In another letter he expressed his thanks to his employers, the Salt Union, for the way in which they had treated the dependants of those who had endured such rough times whilst their loved ones fought in the Battle of the Somme. He wrote, *"Our brigade has had a very rough time in this last three months, with rain, frost and snow, shells, bullets and mines, it has been a terror. The first trenches I was in were only 35 yards from the huns. We caught a squad of them working in the rear of their trench. We soon downed them, but the others spotted us and rattled at us for 48 hours. We dared not show out heads above the trench. We also have been acting as guide to a certain trench. It is a very risky job, running about all night while bullets are coming from all directions. One night the other guide with me got wounded, so it gave me double work. The officer wanted a message taking while I was away, so an N.C.O took it. When I got back the officer was uneasy because the N.C.O had not returned. I went to the place he had been sent to, and they told me he had to go through two woods and it was very dark. I turned out and went to look for him, I took the turn he would have done had he gone wrong, and went searching about. After going about 2,000 yards I stepped through a gap in the hedge and got a nice shock. Lying on the ground about a yard from me were three huns with helmets, rifles and full kit. I whipped my rifle from my shoulder and butt ended it, meaning to have a good do for it. I noticed they did not move, so I stepped closer in and saw the frost on their packs. Then I knew they were dead. My first thought was souvenirs. I got in between them and was going to collect something when a star shell went up. I soon found where I was, I had got between our lines and the huns. They spotted me, opened rapid fire, and sent light after light up. I flung myself into the ditch and waited about ten minutes. I don't know how I escaped being hit, for the bullets struck all around me. All thought of souvenirs had gone out of my head. When they ceased I made a sprint for it."* Todger survived this latest skirmish and eventually found the missing N.C.O.

The Battle of Guillemont

In another letter Todger vividly tells of the battle for Guillemont, which for the 1st battalion was more accurately an attack on Falfemont Farm. There had been almost continuous fighting in the area from July 1916 but it was not until the intervention of Todger's division that it was finally taken on the 3rd September. Over the months the allies had been beaten back from taking Guillemont on no fewer than four occasions. To approach the village meant exposure to bare country where the Germans had excellent observation. The enemy had converted the village into a fortress with a chain of dugouts and tunnels that defied the heaviest artillery barrages. In the first attack a lack of artillery had hampered the allied advance and on another occasion the crossfire of machine guns and uncut wire had brought the advance to an end. It was then the turn in August of a division that included three battalions of the Royal Fusiliers, the 1st Kings, 17th Middlesex and 13th Essex in its assault but yet again they were beaten back. However, despite these failings Guillemont exposed true heroism and three V.C's were won in its assault. The village was eventually taken by a combination of divisions, which included the support of the Cheshires. The whole British line was able to push forward beyond the village, capturing Falfemont Farm and Ginchy.

Todger Jones wrote his own thoughts on his division's intervention in a letter to his parents, *"The next stumbling block to our advance was Guillemont, Mouquet Farm, and the surrounding stronghold. They (the Germans) had beaten back all attempts to take it from them. Division after division had tried to wrest it and tried in vain. Then they brought our division, and they told us again that we had been brought to do what others had failed to do. I am proud to know that I belong to the brigade and regiment that did it. It was a terrific struggle, and we were repulsed four times. Our company and platoon had to take the lead on the fifth charge. The bombers won through and leaped in the trench. We knocked the machine gunners over, and helped the following waves to get through with little loss. It was a terrible journey, the worst I have been through yet. It was there I had a good do, a wild three minutes. We got rid of those about us, and I rushed in the next traverse and met a big chap full of fight. He made for me with the bayonet, but I know too many tricks for any Prussian guard and I soon crushed him out. I have a souvenir of the fight with him, it fell from his inside pocket as he dropped, it is a first class iron cross. We lost all our officers in this advance, but we had won and removed the stumbling block. We were then reinforced, and advanced another 3,000 yards past Guillemont and dug in, being too weak to go any further. We stayed there until relieved in the early morning. We went into support about 600 yards behind, and shelling was very heavy. It was here that I got wounded."* This was on the 5th September and Todger continues, *"A party was lost and I told them I could take them down for a drink, as they had been without food or water for over 60 hours. I got them to the place they had to stay at, and was making my way back when one of their big ones dropped alongside and lifted me about ten yards, a piece getting me in the right shoulder and leg. I refused to go down the line, and one of our medical officers, a hero, is doing fine with me. My arm was useless for a day or two, but is doing well now. I am trying to get the cross and some photos home, and you can show them to the lads at the club and the works."* After Guillemont Todger's battalion spent a week holding the line on the right of the attack on the Flers-Courcelette line, before getting ready for their next attack, the village of Morval.

Meanwhile on the 15th September the British introduced a new weapon into the conflict. The War Office had sponsored the construction of a machine that could cross trenches and was both armed and armoured. The national news press gave it various names including 'flat-footed monster' but it became commonly known as the 'tank' because of its resemblance to a water tank. It was still relatively untested and liable to such a frequency of breaking down that only 32 could be dispersed across the front. However, its immediate effect was sensational. The bewildered Germans, on seeing these flat-footed monsters, were forced to retreat providing that day the greatest forward advance yet seen in the war.

Todger Jones standing over the body of a Prussian Guard after he had taken his Iron Cross. He later told a reporter, "Next to the V.C, I think more of that Iron Cross than all the rest, and God knows how much I appreciate all that my fellow townsmen have done for me. But it's quite another story. I won that cross in a single-handed joust with a company commander of the First Prussian Guards. And I don't think the poor chap had ever had the chance to wear it. But he had to go, for there was only him and me for it. He made for me with a bayonet, but I knew too many tricks even for a Prussian Guard, and I soon settled him. The Iron Cross, in its little case, fell from his inside pocket as he dropped. It's new, I suppose he'd just received it from the Kaiser."

The attack on Morval

"It is a story that will live, a record of dauntless pluck and unfailing cheerfulness in the face of death and has no parallel in the glorious history of the Victoria Cross."

A.E. Littler's description of Todger Jones
in the World Wide Magazine (1917)

On the 25th September 1916 began an Allied attack on the whole front from Martinpuich to the River Somme. The specific objective for the British was to capture the area to the north of Flers to a point midway between the village and Martinpuich. It was also intended that the British would capture the villages of Gueudecourt, Lesboeufs and Morval.

The worn out 5th division, which included Todger's battalion, had already suffered a lot of severe fighting and heavy casualties to date. Indeed, Todger Jones was still recovering from his own battlefield injuries when his division were given their fresh objective, the capture of Morval on the Morval-Lesboeufs line. As Gerald Gliddon describes in his definitive account of the Battle of the Somme, it would be a difficult task, *"With its commanding position and a well fortified line of trenches in front of it facing the Allies it was always going to be a very difficult village to capture. In addition there were numerous sunken roads in the area and timbered ravines which were all carefully fortified."* It was planned that the 5th division would attack Morval with the divisions 16th and 95th brigades taking the lead in the attack, supported with three of the new 'tanks'. However, it was the 15th brigade, which included Todger's battalion who forced their way through the fortified German lines and mopped up the dugouts and cellars in the village, capturing five machine guns in the process. The troops then moved out into open country to the east of Morval.

The battle scene at Morval on the 25th September 1916. The British attacked in three pre-planned stages. During the intervals time was taken to organise the battalions to go forward with the barrage. Three tanks then followed, mopping up German trenches south west of the village. The whole attack went well, so well that it took just 13 minutes to push through the village and reach the eastern exits of Morval. The Cheshires began consolidating their position here about 3pm and it was then that Todger pulled off his daring deed.

Digging

It was on the first day of the attack, after having secured this stronghold village, and whilst they were consolidating their defences to the village that Todger Jones undertook the remarkable feat of bravery that was to gain him the Victoria Cross. Todger's company is said to have advanced, and whilst still under incessant sniper fire, their commander gave instructions to start digging themselves in with spades. No orders had been given to assault the German lines beyond Morval and it is reputed that Todger, amidst such mayhem made pleas to the officer to attack but these were declined. Bullets continued flying, and after one close shave Jones retorted to his officer, *"If I am going to die, it will be fighting, not digging."* He had just witnessed the shooting of 18-year-old runner Pte George Kenworthy who had been killed whilst digging next to him. Todger threw down his entrenchment tools, picked up his rifle and charged into the battlefield, alone and still under sniper fire from the enemy trenches. On his drive across 200 yards of enemy lines, he returned shots against a sniper up a tree and killed him. Undaunted and still underfire he carried on and despatched another two snipers before reaching the German trenches. On his advance one bullet had passed through his helmet and another through his coat but undaunted, Todger returned fire, killing one soldier who lurched at him with a fixed bayonet, before the remnants of the demoralised German line dived into a dugout. He had expended his grenades earlier and helped himself to an enemy stick grenade, throwing it into the trench after the German soldiers. He killed another three before an extremely frightened soldier climbed out of the dugout and intimated in broken English that they wished to surrender.

An illustration from 1917 showing Todger with his prisoners.

An official war photographer captures one of the most remarkable events in the First World War. It shows Todger's prisoners being marched to gaol. This photograph was later presented to him and hung for many years on his wall at Princess Street.

Troops move up to attack in the Battle of Morval.

A view of the devastated village of Morval as it appeared on the day Todger Jones captured his prisoners.

Ruins in Morval. At least one man could find some rest amongst the devastation.

Todger ordered them to come out, one by one, stipulating that if any man carried a weapon he would be shot. To his disbelief over a hundred soldiers, together with their officers, came out with their hands above their heads. Todger later remarked in a press interview, *"Up went their hands and I laughed like blazes. It fairly tickled me to death, that did, and I couldn't stop laughing. Why? Well, a bit of fun I once saw at a pantomime flashed through my mind. A comedian, who played the part of the squire, revolver in hand, rounded up all the servants, butlers and gardeners and up went their hands. Then he came to the grandfather clock, pointed his revolver at it, shouting 'Hands Up!' and immediately the hands of the clock whizzed around. Well I tell you I roared with laughter at the thought coming into my mind at such a time, when I was playing a lone hand, for it looked so comical to see them all with their hands up."* After about ten minutes Todger was joined at the German trenches by a sergeant and fellow soldier, and proceeded to return his bounty of prisoners back to British lines.

Todger wrote home to his Mother with his account of the goings on near Morval. He had twice been in serious conflicts in recent weeks and on the second occasion, prior to the attack on Morval, had sustained injuries as a shell lifted him ten yards into the air. It left pieces of shrapnel in his shoulder but Todger had adamantly refused to go into hospital and stuck with his duty to the battalion. However, it was the immediate cause for his concern in his letter, probably to allay his mother's fears. He wrote, *"My wound is nearly better, it was in the shoulder and I would not leave the battalion. I have been in action twice since, and God again has cared for me and got me through all dangers. It seems as though your prayers for my safety have been more than answered."* Turning to the incident for which he was about to win the V.C, Todger commented, *"In our last action when we took certain villages I was extremely lucky we had taken a position and were taking another, and I felt the bullets passing me. I knew they would get me if something was not done, so I went across. While going one bullet passed though my steel helmet and four more through my jacket, when I got through I soon settled them. Some of them shouted at me from their dug out entrance until I settled accounts with them. The rest was easy, they started flinging their arms up, and I soon got the fear of God into them.*

Two of my chums came across and helped to get them away to our lines. We took 150 back with us, I got a little shrapnel wound in the neck in one barrage, but it was not much and is all right now." Todger's estimate of 150 is far higher than the official figure of 102 prisoners which is always quoted. It appears that many prisoners were killed on his return to British lines. In his interview with A. E. Littler in 1917 Todger explained, *"The official report speaks of me bringing in a hundred and two, but, though I didn't check their numbers, there must have been nearly a hundred and fifty of them when I got them in to the open, including four or five officers and any number of non-coms, or whatever the Germans call them. But before we got into our lines, over forty of them were killed by our shells, which were sweeping the ground."*

First News

First news of the 36-year-olds bravery hit the headlines in the national and local press on the 27th October 1916, more than a month after the event. The face of Pte. T. A. Jones adorned the front of the *Daily Mirror* and news of his deed appeared in every other national newspaper. Locally, the *Runcorn Weekly News'* front page headlines and sub headings read, *'Runcorn soldier awarded the Victoria Cross. Honour for Private T.A.Jones. First V.C in the Cheshire Regiment. Attacked dug-out and captured a Hundred Prisoners'*. The report read, *"Yesterday (Thursday) widespread gratification was occasioned in Runcorn by the receipt of the news that a Runcorn soldier, Private Thomas Alfred Jones had been awarded the Victoria Cross. Private Jones is on turn for early leave from the front, and may be expected within a week or two. During his leave it is probable that he will be invested by his Majesty the King at Buckingham Palace. It is almost certain that a reception for the hero will be arranged locally. The first intimation of the news came from Chester Castle. Private Findlow, a member of the Military staff at Chester, was sent by the officers of the Cheshire Regiment with the news to the parents of Private Jones. As Jones is the first member of the Cheshire Regiment to have won the great hallmark of brave deeds, the congratulations which accompanied the message were doubtless both hearty and sincere. The news was confirmed later by a message from the Records Office at Shrewsbury. To the many Runcornians who know Jones the news was a pleasure without being a surprise, most of them regarded the recipient as belonging to the type of man who shows great personal coolness and courage in positions of danger. In addition it was generally known that Private Jones had already distinguished himself by daring deeds and had been somewhat unfortunate, in so much as several officers who had noted his courage and had informed him he would be recommended for honours were killed before the opportunity of doing so arose."*

The *Runcorn Weekly News* continues, *"The exact details as to the deed of bravery for which Private Jones was accorded the cross are not yet forthcoming. So far as can be ascertained, however, it seems that when out with a bombing party he attacked a German dug out single handed and reduced the occupants to a state of terror, with the result that when reinforced by two of his chums he was able to take 100 prisoners back into the British lines. This amazing feat is the more remarkable from the fact that Jones was then recovering from the effect of a wound."* The paper was keen to give a sketch as to Jones character. It continued, *"Private Jones is of rather spare build, of medium height, and of a cold phlegmatic temperament which makes an ideal soldier for the trench warfare so much in evidence at the present time. He has always been known amongst his companions for his cool temperament in all sorts of disturbing circumstances."*

Todger survived the four-day assault on Morval, which for his battalion would be their last sight of the Somme. Colonel Crookenden explains in his book on the history of the Cheshire Regiment in the Great War, *"On relief, the 1st Battalion moved to the Citadel, north of Bray and thence by train to S.E of Abberville. Though the Somme battle continued well into the winter months, they had seen the last of it."* Through the heroism of infantrymen like Todger the battalion had their good share of the reputation gained by the division.

Tributes to Todger

*"Sigh not the old heroic ages past
the times in which we live are big with fate
and heroes creep upon the scene.
Right in the front rank of these heroes stand Private T.A. Jones."*

– Sir Frederick Norman (1916)

As Todger's fortnight of leave from the front approached in November 1916 the excitement of Runcorn's townsfolk was beginning to reach fever pitch. Congratulations were pouring into his parents' family home at Princess Street. *The Runcorn Weekly News* recorded on the 3rd November 1916, *"Since the receipt of the news that their son had been granted the Victoria Cross, Mr & Mrs Jones, of Princess Street, have been overwhelmed with messages of congratulation, verbal, by letter and wire. When Private Thomas Alfred Jones obtains the leave to which so many people are looking forward, he may, should he chose, spend a few hours answering communication expressing the hearty good wishes of relatives and friends, even of persons who have no acquaintance with him but appreciate his gallant deeds. Meanwhile Runcorn deeply feels the honour that has fallen to the lot of one of her sons and many inquires are being made as to*

Todger shows his bullet-ridden steel Brodie helmet to his parents.

An artist's impression by Arch Webb in the World Wide Magazine showing Todger after having entered enemy trenches. Two of the snipers who had being shooting at him had been displaying the white flag.

the date of the hero's return. Rumours were circulated in the town on Tuesday to the effect that he was due home immediately, but none were based on fact. The only communication his parents have had from him since the announcement of the award was a field card on Tuesday morning, stating he was quite well and was writing further."

Flags were flown in honour of Jones at the Town Hall and the Liberal Club, where he had been a well-known and popular member. At a meeting of the Runcorn Urban District Council it was resolved, *"that the hearty congratulations of the Council be tendered to Private Thomas Alfred Jones V.C, on the distinguished honour conferred upon him. The Council on behalf of his fellow townsmen desires also to express its high appreciation of his valour which adds a lustre to the records of the Town, as well as to the County Palatine, this being the first V.C, conferred during the present war on any member of the Cheshire Regiment."* The Council debated Todger's achievements with some pride and, in his closing address, the Chairman of the Council remarked that Todger had brought a fame to this town that had not existed since a Runcorn man carried the standard into the Battle of Agincourt almost 500 years earlier. The Council hurriedly convened a special meeting of the great and the good in the district to take place that week at the Technical School. There would be just one item for consideration at this meeting, how should the town

A copy of the magnificent illuminated scroll that was presented to Todger by the Runcorn UD Council. The original scroll is now exhibited in the Mayor's Parlour at Runcorn Town Hall. A copy of the 2ft scroll is displayed at the Cheshire Military Museum.

recognise its hero son? They considered buying the deeds to his parents' house or awarding Todger a substantial sum in treasury bonds or war savings certificates but army rules prevented financial incentives from being given to servicemen. However, that did not deter the Salt Union works from awarding his parents an annuity of fifty pounds per year.

Letters

Amongst the mass of letters received, some from autograph hunters, was one from Mr J. F. L. Brunner M.P for the Northwich constituency, which followed an earlier telegram. It read, *"Dear Mr & Mrs Jones, I sent you a telegram last night to congratulate you on the success of your son winning the highest honour a British soldier can get. Mrs Brunner and Sir John, join with me. It is a great joy to us to think that a Runcorn man has done so well. His native town will be very proud of him. I hope soon to have the pleasure of shaking hands with him. When you see him tell him that we send our hearty congratulations and wish him the best of good luck. Yours sincerely, J. F .L Brunner"*. Sir Frederick Norman, a distinguished gentleman of the district wrote, *"Only a private, remember, but stamped with the hallmark of heroism for which many a Field Marshal would gladly give his baton. I swell with pride when I think that a Runcorn lad has won such glorious renown, and that pride is all the greater when I remember that the man who bred him has been my lifelong friend."* Other messages of congratulations came from officers of the Cheshire Regiment, and Mr Holford of Winsford, in whose office Private Jones served as a lad. Perhaps the most significant letter of the week came from Quarter Master Sergeant Noble who enclosed *'some of the correct ribbon to be worn with the Victoria Cross, and also giving specific instruction as to the correct way of wearing the decoration upon the tunic.'*

Mrs Jones received a letter from Captain G.F.Ashton, who formerly commanded Todger in the Runcorn Volunteers and who was then himself on active service. He wrote, *"Dear Mrs Jones, I have received from Major Timmins a newspaper cutting describing the wonderful bravery of your son, for which he has received the Victoria Cross. Runcorn will feel justly proud of being able to claim a man who has done one of the most gallant deeds of the war as a townsman. Personally I feel a special pride and delight in the fact that he is an old Runcorn Volunteer and served at a time when I was in command. I trust his courageous accomplishment will be recorded on the walls of the Drill Hall as an incentive to brave actions by other men of the present and future generations. You must be a very proud mother, and I congratulate you on possessing such a son."* Major Timmins later called at the Jones family home in Princess Street to congratulate them personally on Todger's achievement.

News of the old boy's bravery was celebrated at the Parish School when the news of his award came through. The union flag was proudly unfurled and flown from the school's flagpole, and it was to remain there for some weeks to come. *The Runcorn Weekly News* recorded, *"The news was given to the boys on Thursday afternoon, and hearty cheers accorded the V.C man."* The Parish Church School had shown a great deal of interest in the endeavours of its old boys. The school praised the gallant deeds of their old boys but took particular pride in the achievements of Todger Jones and, Leonard Pollitt of the 5th Cheshires. He won the Distinguished Conduct Medal after his retrieval of four badly wounded comrades from the battlefield whilst under heavy enemy rifle fire. Indeed he was the first Runcorn man to receive honours in the war and the first soldier in his battalion to be awarded the Distinguished Conduct Medal. The Tzar of Russia later awarded Pollitt the Medal of St George, 3rd class. Not surprisingly the school's Union Jack was hoisted in proud salute of the gallantry shown by Todger, Pollitt and the other local heroes. The Headmaster, Mr Lindsay, wrote to his schoolboys, *"We must pray that*

God will give them all strength to do and to endure all that he wishes; that he will give them victory in battle and a safe return; and that in his own good time he will restore to us again the blessings of peace."

Witness

The circumstances under which Todger Jones had secured the Victoria Cross were later given in a detailed eye-witness account to the *Runcorn Guardian*, fuelling the passionate frenzy that already existed in the town for details of the heroics of the Runcorn infantryman. Sergeant Stretcher told the paper, "What I want you to know about is what happened on September 25th when we took a village. We had advanced rather too quickly and won our objective 20 minutes before time. We started to dig ourselves in as quickly as possible. We were not digging many minutes before bullets began to fly. Jones turned to his officer and said, 'They nearly got me, come on, let's go and get them. There will be trouble for us if we don't'. The officer declined to let him go, and told him to go on digging. We got to work again, and soon two or three bullets whipped past Todger's head. A moment later a chap standing against him got one in the leg. He turned to the officer and said 'If I've got to be killed I'll be killed fighting, not digging a hole' and off he went on his own. The lads thought it was the last of him, as our barrage was very heavy on the place he was going. We watched, every second expecting him to go down, until he jumped into the trench. Some said 'poor old man'. They saw the huns jumping about and thought they had got him. Seven or eight minutes afterwards two more of his chums came up and when they heard what had happened they said, 'If Todger is over there we are going after him'. Two more joined them and they went across. This is what they found. There was Todger standing by over a hundred Germans in a big hollow, he was ordering them to put on their coats, with his pals he rounded them up and brought back over a hundred, including a general staff officer. After a while we got out of him a little of what happened. As he went over a bullet went through his helmet and three through his coat, but he took no notice. When he got to the trench he got three of them straight away, and started to settle them as he met them. They bolted into their dug out and commenced to pop at him from the doorway. He got all of them that tried to get him. He flung a bomb down the nearest dug-out, and three came running out with their hands up. Todger asked if any spoke English, and one said he could, so he told them they could either be taken prisoner or be killed. He added he would prefer to kill them. He told one of the Germans to tell his mates to come out of the dugout one at a time and any man who came out with arms would be shot. They came out, and when his chums came across they said it was the finest sight they had ever seen. I tell you there was a shout went up when Todger led his prisoners into our lines. They say eleven officers recommended him for the Victoria Cross. He is 'Top Hole'. He has earned it many a time, but has been unlucky in that the people who count were not there at the time."

The Cheshire regiment magazine the 'Oak Tree' paid its own tribute to Private Jones. It describes the plucky deeds of Todger and explains, "He has throughout his time at the front shown in endless instances a devil-me-care contempt for danger, and has performed very many acts of gallantry. His 'drumming up' (making tea) for the men of company while under a hot fire from the Hun trenches is one instance of his coolness. Owing to a mishap to his rifle he made tea and took it around to buck them up. Somehow he always succeeded in having a fire on which to cook anything that was going. On one occasion, at night, about 50 men of another regiment had lost their way under a heavy fire. Jones happened to be returning from the trenches, he met those 50 men and guided them to safety. He was always cheerful and happy, and his good spirits kept the men lively."

A HERO COMES HOME

*"Runcorn is smiling through its tears today
Its clouds have vanished and its skies are Blue
For you have turned to brightness all its grey
Brave 'Todger' Jones – the shouts are all for you."*

**From a poem by J. J. Freeland
of Leicestershire 1916**

On the 9th November 1916 Todger Jones returned to Runcorn for two weeks' leave from the front. The war hero received the kind of welcome that has only ever been afforded to royalty. *The Runcorn Weekly News* described the public response, *"Yesterday (Thursday) was a great day in the history of Runcorn, for it witnessed the homecoming of Private Tom Jones, V.C the first lad in Runcorn to win the coveted honour as well as the first lad in the Cheshire Regiment. To say that Runcorn was wild with enthusiasm is but to describe the scenes in the mildest possible manner, for the whole town combined in one huge burst of enthusiasm and joyous welcome, and its warmth was all the more marked in as much as the notice of his coming was so short. It was generally anticipated that he would leave France on the 17th, and the arrangements for his reception were being made for about that time. In the middle of Thursday morning, however, a telegram handed in at Euston by Jones himself reached his parents, informing them that he hoped to arrive home by the 2-55 at Runcorn Station."* The news spread across the town like wildfire and within hours Runcorn had put on a festive appearance with flags, banners and bunting appearing in the streets. By lunchtime Devonshire Square, Regent Street and Princess Street

Family and friends hail the Runcorn war hero at the back of his Princess Street home. Todger's father is in the far left of the picture.

Everywhere Todger went he was accompanied by curious onlookers, keen to congratulate the first celebrated local soldier in 500 years.

The Daily Sketch heralds the home-coming of Todger Jones, V.C.

were a mass of colour and areas further afield well decorated. Runcorn Urban District Council had been busily involved in their preparations for his homecoming, which now needed to be brought forward. *The Runcorn Guardian* continues the story, "*The whole town was agog with excitement. The news had been announced at the schools, and the dismissal of the youngsters at noon and the outburst of their youthful exuberance added liveliness to the already existing enthusiasm. At home the parents were kept quite busily employed attending to the numerous callers, and their pride in their boy appeared to increase as the time for his arrival drew near. School children were keen purchasers of all kinds of flags with which to wave their signals of welcome at the soldier hero.*"

Crowds

Groups of children wandered the streets carrying their flags and singing patriotic songs. Many of the town's works had, like the schools, offered their workers a half-day holiday. Crowds assembled at the station and by three o'clock Lowlands Road, Station Road and the surrounding fields were reputed to be packed with thousands of people in scenes that were unprecedented in Runcorn. Todger's parents were conveyed to the station in Sir Frederick Norman's motor car. The Jones family, his friends and civic guests gathered at the station platform. Another prominent guest at the station was Mr Malcolm, the Managing Director of the Salt Union where Todger had worked before joining the forces, Major Timmins, and Platoon Commander Jas Beck represented the Runcorn detachment of the Cheshire Volunteers. The Highfield Band kept the expectant party in festive cheer whilst the V.C hero, unexpectant of the reception that was about to greet him made his way from London. *The Runcorn Weekly News* again takes up the story, "*As the train steamed into the station some minutes late a great cheer was given as the V.C hero was recognised through the carriage window. He was accompanied by two of his nephews, who had been to Crewe to meet him, and they carried his equipment, including his steel helmet pierced by the bullet which caused him to go for the enemy in such daring fashion. He was literally dragged from the train by admirers to where his parents awaited him, and happy was the meeting between the old couple and their hero son. The family were accommodated in one of the waiting rooms where the family reunion took place. As Private Jones reached the exit from the station he was met by the Chairman of the Council and others, who welcomed him to his native heath. He had no sooner emerged from the station than great cheers rent the air as the hero of the hour was*

Four heroes in the forecourt of Buckingham Palace, pictured after King George V had presented each soldier with the Victoria Cross. From left to right, Sgt. Davies; Pte. T. A. Jones; Sgt. Saunders; and Pte. Hill.

24

Wounded soldiers from the Vicarage and Cottage Hospitals in Runcorn congratulate Todger on his arrival back in town.

observed, accompanied by Mr Smith and Mr Taylor, while his parents and relatives were accommodated in Sir Frederick Norman's car. Hardly had Jones got out of the station before his hand was seized first on one side and then the other until it was impossible to make progress, so keen was the competition to greet him. After being conveyed a short distance shoulder high he persuaded his bearers to allow him to walk and he managed to reach Devonshire Square, but here the pressure of the crowd drove him a short distance along High Street instead of Regent Street, in which direction his home lay."

By all accounts Todger Jones was both overwhelmed and embarrassed at the rapturous reception and the outpouring of euphoria that greeted him. The police and soldiers had to clear a passage to allow Todger to move. However, he managed to find a seat in the car as it approached. The vehicle continued slowly in the direction of the family home at Princess Street but not before Mr Smith, from the Council, jumped on board the car footplate and made a brief speech on the town's pride in Todger. This provoked a rapturous response from the thronging crowd. He eventually made it home through the back alleyway to the house and appeared in the front bedroom window of his home where he received the applause of the crowd, before calling for cheers for the men still in the trenches. After an afternoon spent greeting friends and relatives he could finally relax. It is questionable whether Runcorn has ever witnessed scenes like those given to Todger Jones, either before or after.

The following morning the British press covered the homecoming of the local hero with glowing tributes. *The Daily Sketch,* one of the leading daily papers of the time, carried photographs of Todger's astonishing reception across their front page. They hailed Pte. Jones as the first local soldier to bring distinction and honour to his town since Agincourt – 500 years earlier. Sir Frederick Norman was bowled over by the attention given to the local lad and the status he had achieved for his hometown, *"Runcorn had proud traditions in the past, her sons had won honourable mention in art, medicine, and in the law, and now this modest lad from Princess Street went and hurled them on to the pinnacle of renown and associated their town with a fearless patriotism that would take a Redtail all life to keep up with."*

Footnote: *Redtail was a term occasionally used to describe a citizen of Runcorn. It is believed to have originated from an old coat of arms for the town that showed a red cat's claw with two tails either side. The schooner 'Redtail' was launched at Runcorn in 1867. It showed the emblem of the cat's claw and red tail on the stern of the ship.*

Wild celebrations greeted Todger in Devonshire Square. The schools and works of his native town were closed in honour of his arrival home.

Visits

During his fortnight's leave Todger twice visited his old school at the request of its scholars, since they had shown great enthusiasm to see him, and he was given a rapturous welcome. On his arrival, Mr Lindsay, the Headmaster who had taught him many years earlier greeted him and introduced Todger to the boys. He then presented the school's Vere Foster prizes and certificates. This was an annual award for handwriting for which the Parish School was well known. Mr Lindsay wrote of the occasion in the school logbook, *"He (Jones) spoke to the boys of the points of character evidenced in his noble deed. After the presentation of prizes, Mr Smith, who taught in this school during the time that Tom Jones was in attendance, gave him a solid silver cigarette case bearing his monogram and the following inscription 'Pte Thomas Jones, V.C. Old Boy – Runcorn Parish Church Boys' School, from the Staff.' Patriotic songs were sung, and the proceedings terminated with Auld Lang Syne."* The school had a special school holiday in Todger's honour and there existed a great deal of pride in this particular old boy's heroic achievements. Later that day he visited the Salt Union works at Weston Point, and accompanied by his brothers and photographers, was given a tour of the works and received an ovation from his former work mates.

On the Saturday he attended a football match between Runcorn and the Salt Union. A church parade was held in his honour at the St Paul's Wesleyan Church on the Sunday. The Highfield Band headed a procession from the Drill Hall in Greenway Road. It consisted of a number of home defence corps, soldiers on leave and the Runcorn detachment of the Cheshire regiment. Todger headed the procession alongside Major Timmins, commanding officer of the Runcorn Volunteer detachment. Old volunteer comrades were invited to supper with Todger the following Thursday night at the Waterloo Hotel. He had been given a variety of gifts during his travels including a gold watch and chain, framed photographs, smoker's cabinet, case of cutlery, field glasses and engraved silver wristwatch. His former employers at the Salt Union had presented him with a silver teapot. He later received a set of cutlery and life membership of the Liberal Club at a smoking concert at the Public Hall, Runcorn.

On Friday 17th November 1916 Todger departed for London to be presented the following day with his Victoria Cross by King George V. Once more he was thrust into the national limelight and appeared in the national press with his V.C along with three other winners. *"How the dickens did you do it, Jones?"* asked King George V when he invested the Cheshire infantryman at Buckingham Palace. Todger later told a magazine, *"I won't tell you what I answered on the spur of the moment but the King laughed. I gave him an idea how the thing had been done, and he laughed again at the thought of me fetching home my happy little family."*

Chester

One of the highlights of Todger's week after his return from London was his triumphal visit to Chester on Monday 20th November. He visited the city with his parents, accompanied once more by Sir Frederick Norman in his motor car. Chester gave him the same bewildering reception as shown in Runcorn. Indeed, the Chester Chronicle declared after his visit, *"Hero-worship is still a living instinct in the hearts of Englishmen. Men, women, boys, and girls lined the pavements in tightly packed crowds, innumerable shoulders and faces were thrust forward over the balconies of the rows, and human figures peered forth from most of the high windows commanding a view of the route. Some of the shops hung out national flags, and many women and children carried patriotic emblems for waving".* On the arrival of Sir Frederick's motor car at the Eastgate of the city it was halted whilst the band and soldiers from the regimental depot organised themselves in processional order behind and around the open-topped vehicle. Todger was simultaneously greeted by Major Husey, and then proceeded the kind of arrival within the Roman walls that would have befitted Caesar.

His escort entered the city and as the car passed through the gates the regimental band struck up, *'See the Conquering Hero Comes.'* It whisked through the thronged streets, the *Chronicle* describes, *"Several soldiers stepped abreast of the car on each side of it, and the general body of the escort, consisting of twenty-three men and three N.C.O's marched in the rear of the car, presently to be joined, in Bridge Street, by the King's School Cadets in their khaki uniforms. The progress through the streets had a right triumphal note about it, and the crowds indulged in the emotion of exuberant patriotism and enthusiasm for the army in a way they had not had an opportunity of doing since – well since perhaps the relief of Mafeking (Boer War), for during this war troops have gone and come through the streets with no ringing cheers and sounds of encouraging greeting."* The crowds in the streets and rows in Eastgate Street and Bridge Street maintained an unbroken roll of cheering. By the time the Castle gates were reached the procession gained a crowd of considerable proportions, jostling for space in the Castle square.

At the Castle yard, in front of the nation's press and cinematographers he was whisked in front of a number of commanding officers and civic dignitaries including the Sheriff of Chester, the Mayor, the Acting-Chief Constable and General Sir William Pitcairn Campbell, the Commander in Chief – western command. It was a particularly solemn occasion for the Mayor of Chester, Alderman Frost, as Todger was one of the last men to have spoken with his son before he was killed in the Somme trenches and the hero brought with him particularly comforting words for the Mayor. Afterwards Todger and his parents were entertained to dinner by the Cheshire regiment, but not before he was photographed, filmed and ceremoniously 'chaired' around the Castle Square by four fellow Cheshires. The latter was something of a tradition for visiting hero troops and in front of large crowds the regimental band hailed the hoisted infantryman with *'For he's a Jolly Good Fellow.'* Afterwards Todger sat down for lunch with his comrades whilst his parents dined with the officers.

Todger spent two other days in Chester whilst on leave. On one day he stayed at the home of his old school friend, Joshua West, and attended at a Buffaloes' Lodge in the Saddle Inn on Grosvenor Road, Chester. The Buffaloes presented him with a silver cigarette tube and case. Afterwards, Joshua West took Todger to a smoking concert of the Chester Glee Club. They played *'See the Conquering Hero Comes'* as he arrived and sang a glee in his honour. The *Chester Chronicle* explained, "Several members of the club and the audience passed their programmes to the hero to obtain his autograph, but this became so general

> *"If I've to die, I'll die fighting, not digging"*.
>
> # PROGRAMME
> — OF —
> ## SMOKING CONCERT
> — AND —
> ## PRESENTATION
> — TO —
> ## PRIVATE T. A. JONES. V.C.
> (Cheshire Regiment).
>
> To commemorate the occasion of his winning the
> — Victoria Cross, —
>
> ## Public Hall, Runcorn,
> SATURDAY. DEC. 2ND. 1916. AT 3 P.M.
>
> Chairman :   Sir FREDERICK NORMAN J.P.

This smoking concert was opened by the male voice choir with 'Rule Britannia' and ended with 'God save the King'.

that someone made the happy suggestion that six-pence for each autograph should be charged, the proceeds to go to one of the soldiers' funds to be selected by Private Jones. The idea was put into execution and a nice little sum was collected as a result." Other out of town visits for Jones during his leave from the front included visits to the Red Cross Hospital and Cable Works at Helsby and Middlewich Town Hall, where he watched a performance of the Highfield Male Voice Choir. The Middlewich Volunteers and local scouts turned up to greet Todger and the customary crowds thronged the area around the Town Hall. He was seen by the whole of Cheshire as one of their own, his name on everyone's lips, and even the Chester volunteers named their Drill Hall cat Todger Jones!

The first great allied offensive in the Somme ended that month, although later in 1918 the Germans were to launch Operation Michael, a frontal assault across a 50-mile line in the Somme. It involved over a million troops and for the Germans was to be their final throw of the dice in an attempt to win the war. However, it failed and a subsequent counter offensive led to the Armistice. The sacrifice in the Somme, on which Todger had fought so courageously, had resulted by moderate estimates, in the loss of 420,000 British soldiers. In all perhaps 1,125,000 perished in this one sombre battleground.

Jones claims to have 'laughed like blazes' when he captured the enemy troops. He recalled seeing a pantomime in which a grandfather clock raised its hands when a gun was pointed towards it.

29

Todger's Interview

Following his return from the front in November 1916 Private T.A Jones, V.C provided a interview to the Runcorn Weekly News on his experiences in France and on the heroism that was widely acclaimed as one of the most daring acts in the war.
The interview is reproduced here in full with the kind permission of the Runcorn & Widnes Weekly News (Chronicle Group Newspapers).

Private Jones's wonderful narrative
"Up went their hands and I laughed like blazes"

In an interview with the representative of the Weekly News last evening, Private Jones told a very graphic story of the feat which won for him the highest distinction to be gained on the field of battle. The incident occurred on the 25th September, when orders were given to take a certain village. They succeeded in this and had got to the edge of a wood outside the village where they were commanded to dig in and consolidate their position. They were engaged in digging themselves in when bullets commenced flying around. "They are going to make it hot for us if we don't reach their position", observed Jones to his officer, "No said the officer, "We can't go for them yet, you get on with your digging." I said, "All right and we went on digging", said Jones.

"The bullets again came flying round, and some of the chaps behind waiting their turn to take the pick and shovel were hit. I looked over the parapet and saw what appeared to be like a white flag. That put the wind in me and said, "See that sir", he said, "Yes", and a few more words. I said "What do you think of that?, let's go and get at them". But he would not allow us, saying he dare not leave that place. "All right" I said, "If I have to be killed I'll die fighting not digging". With that I jumped up and went across and while I was going one bullet went through my steel helmet and four through the side of my tunic. I made for the end of the trench. I remembered my bombing training and that by approaching that way only one at a time can deal with you. Well, three of them came along and I soon put them out and I had my magazine going fairly. Anyhow, they must have had enough, for others behind bolted back into their dug out.

For a minute or two they kept coming to the door of the dug out and having a pop at me, but I was a bit lucky, I suppose. I picked up a bomb and threw it into the dug out and three chaps came out holding up their arms and calling out "Kamerad." I shouted, "What's it going to be? Do you want taking prisoner?" One man who could speak English said, "Yes". I asked him how many were down there, and he replied "about 15". I said "Ask them if they want to be taken prisoner, my mates are coming across and if they find anything wrong with me they will cut you to bits". He went back, and on returning said they were all willing to be made prisoners. I said that anyone who came up with arms or equipment would get shot straight away. I said "Get them out of their dug-out" and that was when the procession started. He, Private Jones, laughed heartily at his recollection of the incident. They came tumbling out of their dug outs, and I should think they were about eight or nine dug-outs altogether. When I got them all lined up I wondered how on earth I was going to get them out of it, and I stood looking at them a bit. I thought some of my mates would be coming in a bit. That is the way with British troops, they won't leave you in a tight corner alone, and we expected another regiment to come up and relieve us any time. To put on the time a bit I told the chap who could speak English that it was very cold where they were going that night and they would take their greatcoats, and I told them to fetch two at a time. They kept going in twos for their mantles, as they call them, and this kept things going for eight or nine minutes.

There was one big fellow I did not like the look of, and when he went for his mantle I kept half an eye on him. When he got to his dug out about 50 yards he made a dash. I whipped round and with a lucky shot made a sieve of him and he rolled over like a rabbit. "Any more of you want to escape?" I turned round and asked the others, but up they swung their hands until I laughed like blazes. I told them to put them down, but they would keep them up. I turned to have a look over the top, and saw some of our chaps coming across, one of them being my best mate, Bogson, and three others. I can tell you my heart went up with a jump when I saw them, and when Bogson came over he says "Hello Todger, what the — — are you doing?" and slapped me across the earhole. Anyhow they helped me to round them up, 150 of them, including a General Staff Officer."

"I suppose the lads raised a yell when they saw you" he was asked. "Yell, you should have heard it", and here Private Jones broke off to speak in the highest possible praise of Bogson. "That chap has deserved recognition hundreds of times. He is a stretcher-bearer, and goes out after wounded many and many a time, and has carried scores of wounded lads in. He risks his life over and over again to save other lads. He deserves something. It is a shame he has not had it before now. He's as brave a fellow as there is in the army. When he knew I had gone across he said, "I'm going after Todger wherever he is, and I'll bring him back alive or dead." I tell you it was grand to see him. When we got then across the officer made me take the prisoners down the line about four or five miles, I was wounded in the shoulder at the time and that made me worse.

"I suppose you have been recommend by a number of officers" was our representative's enquiry. "Yes" was the reply, "There were line regiments on each side of us, and the officers were able to see through their glasses what was going on. They afterwards sent up to find the name of the man who had done it". How Private Jones came to hear of the honour having been conferred on him has its amusing side, showing how little Private Jones estimated what was certainly a most marvellous performance, probably one of the most remarkable in the whole history of the war. "How I got to know of it?" said Private Jones in response to a question. "Well I had completely forgotten it when a chap came to me and said, "Have you a Victoria Cross?" I said "No, but I've an iron cross here I'll sell if your trading." This iron cross, by the way was one Private Jones had picked up, having seen it roll from the pocket of an officer of high rank as he fell, and evidently only just been awarded. Proceeding with his story, he continued, "Well", the chap said, "No I don't mean that. It's quite right". "What are you getting at?" I asked, "Are you potty, hop it my lad" and I left him. I was then met by a Sergeant, who said, "Put it there, my lad" holding out his hand. I said, "What's up with you all this morning?" and he replied "It's alright, my lad, I am right glad to shake hands with you." Well, I went on to the transport Sergeant and asked if there was any mail and he came over to me and said, "Put it there young fellow, and best of luck with you" holding out his hand. "Look here" I said, "Will you tell me what's the matter with you all this morning, I don't know what you're getting at" and for an answer he handed me a telegram from the depot at Chester congratulating me. I knew there was something up. "Hearty congratulations from all ranks at the depot, Chester" was the substance of the telegram. Then I got a notification from headquarters and I realised what it was.

"Were you recognised coming through London?" our representation asked. "No I saw to that" said Private Jones knowingly, "At Euston, though, the stationmaster recognised me and one or two more wanted to know if they could do anything for me". "I surpose you were surprised at the crowds at Runcorn?" he was asked. "What, not half. If I'd known there was going to be such an affair I should have gone round some other way. I'd almost as soon go back to where I came from than face it again." Private Jones spoke of some of the engagements in which he and his regiment had taken part and said they had succeeded where other regiments had failed. He had seen German bodies piled high in front of their lines, and even seen British and German dead lying clutching each others throats or each with their bayonets through the bodies of their opponents.

That the V.C hero has more than a passing thought for the comrades he has left behind is shown in the appeal he made on behalf of the lads of the original expeditionary force. There were not many of them left, he says, and they have been through two winters in the trenches and stood the brunt of Kaiser Bill's first mad rush. He makes an appeal for these lads to be enabled to have a real good rest, for they thoroughly deserve it. It was a pity to see them day after day, week after week, and month after month still pegging at it without any hope of a really good rest and change. For these lads he asks that arrangement should be made for their replacement by other men who have not yet seen the front, and if he were able to carry back good news of this kind he would be almost as pleased as if he were to win further distinction on the battlefield.

Back to the Front

"His example and fearlessness were a fine example to the men".

General Rawlinson
Mentioning Todger Jones in his despatches (1918)

It is difficult to image the horror of the war for serving infantrymen in the Cheshire regiment. The regiment had taken part in some severe fighting since the war began, resulting in the loss of many men. One of the most costly assaults for the regiment had been in the Somme at the frontal attack on Falfemont Farm. In all seven hundred men went over the top in one advance and only two hundred returned, still fit for action. The commanding officer Colonel W.H.G Baker, an Indian cavalryman, congratulated the remnant Cheshires on their success with a ration of rum. The 1st Cheshires and 1st Bedfordshire battalions eventually took the farm on the 5th September 1916.

At times the enemy's troops had fought with stubborn courage, defending every bit of broken woodland and every heap of bricks that was once a building with absolute obstinacy. In March 1917, Todger's Battalion took over a new sector near Cambrai in Flanders. The winter months had been exceptionally cold, and precautions had needed to be taken to avoid 'trench feet'. When in billet men had received hot baths and frequent changes of clothes. Clean socks went up to the front every night and old jam jars filled with grease and a wick, enabled troops to heat food and tea rations. The 1st Battalion was involved with Canadian forces in the attack on Vimy Ridge and the Second Scarpe in April. The battalion was in reserve, but had worked hard in the preparations for battle, carrying supplies and building tracks. It failed to capture the German position, thanks largely to the very heavy belts of wire that the allied artillery was unable to cut.

Arthur dies

'Todger' Jones continued his heroics in the battlefield throughout 1917, without any sense of wanting to avoid the thick of the action. However, his mother had pleaded for him to avoid harm but that was not Todger's style. His family's anxiety was made all the worst by the death of Todger's younger brother Arthur, who died at Runcorn in July 1917 as a consequence of his war wounds. The former Manchester Ship Canal worker had joined the army when war broke out, responding to Kitchener's call to arms at the same time as many of the Highfield tannery workers. The 33-year-old had been shot in the head by a sniper within 24 hours of entering the trenches in

Todger received fan mail and congratulations from across the country, some requesting autographs. This is one of the autographed postcards that well wishers received.

France, and sent to Hampstead Hospital where he had the first of four operations. Arthur Jones was discharged from the army and returned to the company of his parents at Runcorn but never recovered from his injuries.

The battle of Ypres in July 1917 was a long and pressing time for the 22nd (Cheshire) regiment, with several battalions engaged in the four-month conflict. Later on the 26th October Todger's battalion began their moves to capture Polderhoek, in order to create a strong flank for the British battlefront. Afterwards the 1st battalion concluded its service in France for the comparative peacefulness of Italy. To date the battalion which contained the celebrated Runcorn infantryman had partaken in 28 battles, and long periods of trench warfare, yet only once failed in an objective and never lost a trench to the enemy.

1918 was probably the most dramatic and decisive year in the war. In the spring there was a real fear that Britain might have to evacuate her troops from the continent and lose the war against a German foe that still possessed ten million fighting men. The 1st battalion's rather uneventful stay in Italy was brought to an abrupt end by the Germans' great attack on the 5th Army in March 1918. Todger and his fellow Cheshires were hurriedly brought back to France, staying in the Nieppe Forest. In the summer came the great turnaround for the allies, and by the autumn in the constantly shifting kaleidoscope of events the German armies began to retreat on the Western Front. For the first time in the war all the Allied armies on the Western Front from the Meuse to the sea were on the move together, and they continued advancing with short intermissions, either attacking or pursuing, until the end. Previously in isolated set piece offensives at the Somme and elsewhere the Germans had been able to concentrate large forces and employ substantial reserves to parry them. Now the Germans were attacked everywhere at once and their resistance had need to be dispersed.

Todger was making local newspaper headlines again in July 1918. This time it was news of his impending fortnight leave from the front. It had been the first time since his much-heralded return after the award of the Victoria Cross that he had been relieved from this seemingly interminable war. He came home quite unexpectedly from the front only to find his parents were away on holiday. However, explained the *Runcorn Weekly News*, "*But a wire soon brought them back with a resulting warm welcome. Todger has put on weight and looks very much fitter than when he was last in town. He has been on active service about 18 months, returning from Italy to France three months ago. He has little to say concerning his exploits. On Thursday he visited the Drill Hall and inspected the handsome tablet placed there to commemorate what has well been styled 'the greatest individual act of bravery of the war'. He thinks the tablet admirably designed and very artistic. Todger's many friends are determined to make his holiday as pleasant as possible.*" On his return to the front it was back to the Somme for Private Thomas Alfred Jones, returning to the scene of such bitter rivalry in 1916. The Somme ground was scorched by the ruins and had previously been fought over.

Further Honours

In October 1918 it was again rumoured that Todger was being considered for high honours for more unselfish acts of heroism early in September 1918, whilst engaged in capturing the village of Bapaume. The village had been on the battle line as early as August 1914 and after the German push westwards remained in their hands for years. At Bapaume all the buildings had been razed to the ground and several booby-traps and mines left for the advancing allies. Meanwhile, in October, Todger was recuperating in a rest camp after being gassed and slightly wounded in one of the Somme offensives, almost certainly one of the battles being fought to gain the Hindenburg line. For several days he had been blinded by the effects of the gas but recovered his sight. He was still making a speedy recovery when news came through that he was to receive the Distinguished Conduct Medal for his part in the fighting at Bapaume. General Rawlinson announced the award in the following terms, "*This man went forward five times with messages through intense*

Pte. Thomas Alfred Jones, V. C. This official photograph was taken by Mr Chidley's photographic shop in St Werburgh Street, Chester.

sion had failed. Any assembly of the 1st Battalion was difficult and shortness of time, and vigilance by the Germans had made previous reconnaissance impossible. The soldiers had to make the best of the heavy barrage but many soldiers and officers were lost.

The Distinguished Conduct Medal was founded during the Crimean War in 1854 and since 1916 had become the second highest recognition for distinguished conduct in the field after the Victoria Cross. Its award meant that Todger Jones was the most decorated soldier in the history of the 22nd (Cheshire) regiment. In little more than a year he had gained both awards. No other Runcorn man was to gain the Victoria Cross and only six other servicemen from Runcorn gained the Distinguished Conduct Medal during the conflict.

Armistice

News of the Armistice created wild celebrations in Todger's hometown as everywhere else. The intimation of peace came with the sounding of a horn from a ship passing on the Manchester Ship Canal and within a short while all of the buzzers were sounding at works across the district, scores of workers downed tools and walked out without regard for the consequences. The streets were quickly filled and within a short space of time the town was strewn with flags and bunting. However, the majority kept their sense of discipline and remained until the half-day holiday began at noon. It was a short day for the town's school children for they had

barrage of shell and machine gun fire, and delivered most important messages, bringing back an answer to every message. He also led forward stragglers and placed them in position. His fine example and utter fearlessness of danger were a great incentive to the men, and his cheeriness in action was an extremely great asset." The importance of Todger's role can not be overstated. Bapaume was known to be well defended by the Germans and a previous attack by another divi-

only just returned that morning following an epidemic of influenza.

As ever on the scene, the *Runcorn Weekly News* described, "*The bells of the Parish Church were rung at intervals and the whole town seemed to have thronged into the streets dressed in holiday attire. The display of flags, bunting, patriotic mottoes, and gilded relics of the Coronation was a heavy one. Almost every child carried a flag and was decorated with red, white and blue ribbon or rosette. The crowd seemed a trifle in awe by the magnitude of the news.*" Needless to say things were just as lively in the evening as crowds thronged the streets, with revellers at all the places of entertainment. Not everyone would doubtless have been in a frame of mind to celebrate. Mrs Antrobus of Lowes Court, off King Street, Runcorn was a mother who was left to grieve three days before the armistice upon news that her son had been killed. All three of her sons were killed on the front. In the weeks ahead thoughts in Runcorn would turn to what should be done to commemorate the victory over the Kaiser. The War Office Trophies Committee offered the town a machine gun but local people seemed to have had other ideas. One suggestion even being put by Mr Alfred Dodd was that a statue of Todger Jones be erected as the town's war memorial because, "*He is a typical Tommy in face and build.*"

Meanwhile Todger remained on active service on the continent and, during December 1918, in his last publicly issued letter following news of the armistice Todger wrote to his parents, "*I am fairly well and will be alright in a day or two. With you I thank God for his great care and guidance throughout this great struggle and that I can now come home knowing that our cause has been right. When I meet you I can hold up my head proudly and say, "We have won." Many times you have asked me to keep out of danger if I could, but would you in your hearts, have liked me to have done so, are you not now glad that I didn't? Our battalion took part in the last smash that made him throw in the sponge and no wonder, it rained day and night for four days and we advanced about 15 miles. Since the 21st August we have won about 18 decisive battles and advanced about 90 miles. It will be months before we come home, as I think we are going to garrison a German town. We do not realise that the war is over yet, we took it very calmly and have not had the chance to celebrate our victory yet, not by anything with a bit of a kick in it. All the boys are sorry that we were not allowed to bring things home to the swine, that we were forced to halt and be robbed of the soldier's right of sacking and burning, as the Germans did in France and Belgium. Whoever is to blame made a great blunder, as they do not understand the pigs, and think they are lambs we are dealing with. I had a few lucky escapes on the last stunt, Private Evans has got the D.C.M, good luck to him, I suppose you know he was wounded. Tell his sister to let him know we are at Le Quesnoy now, about mid way between Valenciennes and Mons, we have been here for a week. It has snowed today, and been frosty for a week. It is pitiful to see the French prisoners coming back and seeing how their homes have been sacked. Some can hardly stand and look terribly thin and pale. In some of the villages we took the people were nearly frantic and they spoke of the cruel way our prisoners have been treated. It has made us all feel that we want to exterminate them.*" The King, Prince of Wales and Prince Albert paid a visit to the troops at Le Quesnoy on the 3rd December 1918 and were warmly greeted by the 1st battalion, a few days after which the battalion departed for the lines in Italy.

During the entire war, the 1st battalion had never been out of the front line for any period exceeding one month, and on one occasion they had held a sector for 42 days without relief, then a record in either Belgium or France. The Cheshire regiment had developed a proud record but at an enormous cost. Almost eight and a half thousand serving men were killed, but astonishingly, judging by the events described in this book Todger Jones was not amongst those killed. During his 1,391 days of war he had experienced some of the most reckless fighting and brutal battles, yet would be able to return home as one of the most distinguished survivors of the entire war.

On the Home Front

Todger was not alone in his achievements. A second Cheshire had been awarded the Victoria Cross for his deeds of valour in September 1917. Second Lieutenant Hugh Colvin, of the 9th Battalion had received his V.C for courageously commanding two companies under heavy fire at Klien Zollebeke. He had searched enemy dugouts and captured fifty prisoners, then personally wired the front despite heavy fire. After the war the two men were brought together for a picture as they were to be (and still remain) the only two soldiers from the 22nd (Cheshire) regiment ever to win Britain's highest honour for gallantry. Prior to the First World War only 525 British and Commonwealth recipients had been decorated with the Victoria Cross since it was instituted in 1857. Although circumstances have since changed, recipients in Todger's day needed to have officers witness their acts of bravery before an award could be recommended.

The cadre of the 1st battalion of the Cheshire regiment returned to Britain in the spring of 1919. Twenty six surviving men, including Todger, under the command of Captain Sproule M.C returned from France, and after initially being rested at the Catterick barracks, arrived back in Chester on the 25th April 1919. The returning heroes marched through a proud city. They received the warmest of welcomes and their every step back to the Castle was applauded. Their regimental colours were on public display, decorated with oak and acorn wreaths. However, the standard that attracted the most attention was the miniature carried by their celebrated infantryman, Todger Jones. Early in the war the famous miniature standard had been lost behind enemy lines and hidden away for years by local people to prevent it falling into the hands of the Germans. It was returned to the regiment after the final push through Belgium. The Mayor of Chester, Sir John Frost later entertained the men and their officers at the Bars Hotel in Chester. Todger Jones was once more thrust into the limelight with his officers and dignitaries to provide a speech on behalf of the returning Cheshire men. Todger was by now a quite accomplished speaker and he entertained the gathering of the gallant and noble of Chester with his tales of life on the front. He explained that the 1st battalion had not expected such a warm reception on their return home. He added a touch of humour to the proceedings when he recalled how early in the war the troops had been told they were going to Hill 60 *'for a rest.'* This of course was one of the worst battles the battalion had faced, and to some laughter Todger quipped, *"On the Somme it was nice and quiet."*

Following his demobilisation Todger returned

A small sketch showing him playing darts in 1940. It was given to Todger by the unknown artist.

This mark IV tank came to Runcorn in 1920 and was mounted on a plinth at Runcorn Heath. It was intended as a permanent memorial to the war but was scrapped for armaments when war returned in 1939.

to civilian life in Runcorn. For a while attention was still drawn to his wartime fame but over time he managed to avoid any celebrity status. He returned to the Salt Union works at Weston Point, less than two miles from his home, and settled back as best he could into the daily routine of a fitter. The works on the banks of the Manchester Ship Canal came out of the war relatively unscathed, although many of the workmen who had been employed before the war were never to return, their lives having been extinguished in the battlefield. A plant for the vacuum evaporation of brine had been installed at the works in 1911 and loading facilities on the canal front has been improved to allow ocean-going ships to receive salt cargoes. The works were bought by I.C.I in 1937 and continued to produce large quantities of salt, estimated at three-quarters of a million tons a year.

Remembrance

By 1920 Runcorn was finally ready to pay its respects to those who had fought and died in the Great War. The town's War Memorial was officially unveiled on the 14th November 1920 in the presence of 10,000 people. Runcorn had sent 2,000 of its men folk to war, exactly one in nine citizens, and it could now recognise the four hundred local men who had failed to return, giving their lives for the war to end all wars. In addition to Todger forty two other Runcorn men had achieved honours during the war, resulting in six Distinguished Conduct Medals, four Military Crosses, one Distinguished Flying Medal, twenty three Military Medals, three Croix de Guerre and two Russian medals. The Runcorn Liberal Club had a special social evening in 1920 to remember the contribution club members had made to the war effort. Forty war veterans were entertained to tea by Sir John Brunner, after which Sir Frederick Norman presented each of them with a gold medallion. Six presentations were also made posthumously to the families of those Liberal Club members who had made the supreme sacrifice. One of the highlights of the evening was the presentation of the medallion to Todger Jones, who also received a gift of £41 from Sir Frederick Norman. Todger gave a short address during which he urged his fellow Liberals to work on behalf of all those who had suffered during the war.

Later in 1926 The Parish Church School unveiled its own roll of honour board and the name of Todger Jones was amongst those old boys whom the school revered. The school logbook reads, *"The Head Master spoke on the sacrifice of the old scholars who had learnt their first lessons of obedience and good comradeship in the very rooms where they were assembled, alluded to the value of teamwork and its glorious spirit."* Canon Perrin unveiled and dedicated the memorial, after which the scholars sang, *'Fight the good fight.'* Todger commonly paid his own respects to war veterans, and it was not uncommon between the two world wars for him to be

King George V greets Todger Jones during the royal visit to Runcorn in 1925. Standing either side of Todger in the line of introductions are two survivors of Rorke's Drift. To his left is Thomas Taylor and to Todger's right is Thomas Moffatt, whom Todger came to know quite well.

Just a face in the crowd. In 1929 Todger Jones attended a remarkable gathering of VC's at the invitation of the Prince of Wales.

seen at the funerals of Runcorn's war veterans, whether he knew them or not.

King George V made a visit to Runcorn in July 1925 and was presented on his arrival to Todger Jones and two survivors of the 1879 stand at Rorke's Drift when 4,000 Zulus attacked the 150 strong British garrison. The King spent some time chatting with the three men and civic figures before continuing with Lord Derby on his visit through the town. This was the third time that Todger has met the king, the last occasion being in 1920 at a garden party for VC heroes in Buckingham Palace. In 1929 the Prince of Wales (later to become King Edward VIII) invited Todger, and over three hundred other Victoria Cross recipients to attend another reunion at the Royal Gallery in the House of Lords, Westminster. It was a unique national occasion, making headlines and bringing together an astonishing assemble of courageous ex-servicemen. The Victoria Cross recipients received a rapturous welcome from the crowds outside the Houses of Parliament and an even warmer welcome

One of the most decorated figures in the Home Guard during World War Two. A rare view in his Home Guard uniform.

inside from the Prince of Wales. Menus and other things associated with the dinner were signed by many of the men and kept as lasting momentoes. It is believed Todger took with him a tablecloth signed by many V.C heroes but what became of his souvenir is not known. Many of the war heroes stayed in London for the Remembrance Day ceremony and the festival that followed at the Albert Hall. Despite these two royal occasions the 1920s were not an altogether good time for Todger. Three of his brothers died between 1923 and 1926 and following a long illness his mother died in 1927. He remained a committed bachelor all his life but continued to live at the Jones family home, even after his father's subsequent death in 1932.

Some surviving family members still recall that Todger attempted to enlist in the Second

Edward Jones 1842-1932

World War when Britain was plunged into another crisis in September 1939 but he was declined on the basis of his age. The V.C hero's commitment to his country's need had never diminished even in latter years. However, he was accepted into the Home Guard and was posted to key places in the town. Some people recall Todger at the Home Guard post at Runcorn Railway Bridge where he checked papers and ID cards and prevented access to the bridge when the air raid sirens sounded. Others recall him being posted at the post office in High Street. If being 'posted to the post office' was not a strange enough experience for a distinguished Somme veteran, then how must he have felt about using a broom in place of a rifle? It is a matter of some humour that during inspection drills of the Home Guard, there were insufficient rifles with which to parade. It is known that, Todger, arguably the finest and certainly best known marksman that Runcorn had ever produced was provided with a broom handle in place of a rifle. After the war he was invited to attend the Victory Parade at Whitehall and join past and present servicemen for a special dinner at the Dorchester Hotel.

Todger lived a quiet, simple life, keeping himself to himself. He was often seen sitting on his doorstep and about town but always drawing little attention to his renown. He used to rest often at a seat by the swimming baths, and would chat regularly with Thomas Moffatt the elderly veteran of the Zulu attack at Rorke's Drift. However, Todger was always subject to the inquisitiveness of people, particularly young people, unaware of the experiences of his own generation. When pushed he would occasionally talk about the war to children and demonstrate a good sense of humour about his younger days. In private, at home, he played the piano and amongst his favourite old tunes was the Marseillaise. He told stories to his nieces of how as a soldier he would scrounge for food on the front and how he had looked after the youngest members in his platoon, many of whom were 17 or 18 year olds.

Following his retirement from the 'salt works' Todger spent a lot of time visiting the home of his sister, Emily Lightfoot, and became a regular at the New Inn public house in High Street, where his niece was the landlady. From time to time he allowed his stature as a war hero to be revealed. He returned at the invitation of Stephen Davies, Headmaster of the Parish Church Boys' School, to present prizes at the school's annual prize-giving ceremony. It was something that gave him a great sense of pride since Todger had maintained a strong loyalty to his old school.

By 1948 Arthur Bryant in an article in the *Illustrated London News* was enquiring, *'How many Englishmen today. I wonder, remember Todger Jones?'* He continued, *"It is nearly 32 years since this remarkable Englishman and inveterate humorist carried out his great jest which won him the Victoria Cross. I hope the old homeric tale of Todger's doings that day is still told in his old regiment and that he will be honoured there so long as the regiment endures, and that will be to the end of time"*. The regiment did honour Todger, indeed he was a regular guest at regimental functions and had even been given a role in celebrations at the Castle in Chester when the regiment returned home in 1954 from their three year stint in the Middle East.

Prize giving at the Runcorn Parish Church School. Todger presents prizes to winning boys as Headmaster, Mr Davies, looks to the camera.

Lest we forget... Todger Remembered

"His unselfish gift of service enriched everyone and will never be forgotten. We will always hold his memory in our hearts with warm and grateful affection."

Rev. W.F.Good
Chaplain to the British Legion (Runcorn Branch) 1956

Todger Jones died on the afternoon of the 30th January 1956 at Runcorn Cottage Hospital. He had been admitted almost four weeks earlier suffering with heart problems. News of his death was met with great sadness and widespread tributes were given for the retired fitter. Later that week the newspaper headlines read 'His name's on the roll of the brave.' The flags at Runcorn Town Hall and the Parish Church Schools were flown at half-mast, more than 60 years after he had spent his boyhood days within its lofty classrooms.

He is buried in the Jones family grave at Runcorn's Greenway Road cemetery, less than half a mile from where he was born and lived all his life. At his funeral many thousands paid their last respects. The Runcorn Weekly News read, *"To show their sense of bereavement, the townspeople, young and old, lined the whole route as the cortege moved from the home in Princess Street – where he lived with his sister – to St Michael's Church where there was a full congregation to take part in the service. The coffin, draped in the Union Jack, was surmounted by a cushion upon which lay the military medals of this 76-year-old soldier, including the Victoria Cross"* The report continues, *"In the sad parade were civic leaders, including the Chairman of the Council and the Town Clerk, colleagues of the British Legion, representatives of the towns pre-service youth organisations and detachments from the Depot and from every battalion of the Cheshire regiment."* Amongst those assembled was Colonel Newington, Major Sharpley and several other senior officers from the 22nd

A photographic portrait of Todger Jones late in his life. His medals are from left to right; Victoria Cross, Distinguished Conduct Medal, 1914-15 Star, British War Medal and the Victory Medal. The latter trio of medals were awarded to most servicemen and became known as 'Pip, Squeak and Wilfred.'

The Victoria Memorial Hospital at Runcorn or 'Cottage Hospital' as it was more commonly known. Todger Jones died here in January 1956.

the service in the packed church the coffin of Todger Jones was carried the short distance, across Greenway Road, to the Jones family graveside. Here he was laid to rest with full military honours, an event captured on film for cinema-goers. The 22nd (Cheshire) regiment later erected a white marble memorial stone at his graveside. It is shaped in the form of the Victoria Cross and is emblazoned *'For Valour.'*

Shortly after his death Todger's medals, bullet-marked helmet and other war momentoes were presented to the Cheshire Military Museum at Chester by his sister, Emily Lightfoot. His family's wish was that Todger's most important belongings be kept by the regiment for dis-

The funeral cortege on its way to St Michael's Church, Runcorn.

(Cheshire) regiment, Denis Vosper M.P and teachers and pupils from the Parish Church School.

Full honours

At the service Rev.Good, chaplain to the Runcorn Branch of the British Legion said, *"Those of us, who knew Tom Jones, knew him as a kindly and quiet man – a retiring sort of fellow, never willing to put himself into the limelight. He always thought of himself last. Knowing that, we can understand how it was that in the First World War he won the supreme honour of the V.C."* After

Lasting Memory. The Mayor and Mayoress of Halton join Joe Darlington, Percy Dunbavand and flag bearer Norman Neale at the unveiling of the town centre plaque in 2000.

42

play purposes and permanent preservation. In doing so it has allowed new generations to learn of Todger's War. They are one of the most interesting exhibits of the museum and thousands of visitors still marvel at his valour.

His family home was swept away in the early 1960s, as part of the Runcorn town centre re-development and the site is now a car park. Many other places associated with Todger's life have disappeared along with the passing of time, including Hazelhurst's, and the Liberal Club. His old school was demolished but rebuilt as a modern one-storey building close to the same site. The 175th anniversary of the school was held in 1987 and festivities included children dressing in period costumes and displays on their most famous ex-pupil.

Plaques

The commemorative plaque that had been installed in the Drill Hall at Greenway Road went missing at some point over the passing decades. The 5ft by 3ft bronze plaque was re-discovered by chance at the hall just prior to the closure of the building. The Weston & Weston Point British Legion Club had a memorial plaque at their Weston Road club but when it succumbed to closure the Runcorn & Weston Branch of the British Legion decided to present the memorial tablet to the combined Cheshire & Manchester regiment barracks at Warrington. He is also remembered in a commemorative plaque on the floor of the regimental Chapel of St George in Chester Cathedral.

The last resting place of Cheshire's most distinguished soldier. The white marble cross was erected by the Cheshire regiment in front of the Jones family gravestone at Runcorn's Greenway Road Cemetery. The grave was restored in the 1980s after it had deteriorated into a state of neglect.

Another reminder of Todger's memory, not commonly realised by people, is the naming of Morval Crescent in Runcorn. When the Runcorn Urban District Council looked to build the new 'town hall estate' on the Grange it was agreed that one road be named Morval, after the small village in France where he had won his Victoria Cross. In 2000, Halton Borough Council decided to mark the second millennium with the unveiling of a plaque on the wall of the Halton Partnership Centre in High Street, Runcorn. The occasion was attended by the Mayor of Halton, Councillor Bob Gilligan, representatives of Todger's surviving family and the Runcorn & Weston British Legion. The Frodsham Silver Band movingly played the last post at the ceremony.

Stories of this local hero still appear from time to time in the local press, and there are a few older people who can recall Todger later in his life. His name also lives on with the Todger Jones Bowls Trophy. The bowls competition used to be held every year during Todger's lifetime but over time was discontinued. In 1997 the British Legion decided to revive the competition and is now held on the 25th September between teams from two local British Legion branches. They have even added an annual darts competition. The original Todger Jones Bowls Trophy is held at the Cheshire Military Museum and bowlers now compete for a new trophy. Tales of the celebrated soldier from the Somme have never been forgotten, particularly on Remembrance Day when British Legion officials usually make an annual visit to his graveside. However, perhaps the greatest symbol to his bravery and those who fought alongside him rests not in Runcorn or Chester but hundreds of miles away in the former battlefields of France and Belgium. Six hundred commonwealth war cemeteries are testament to the lost generation who fought with him and through the mind's eye those who walk the battlefields today can still glimpse the magnitude and severity of their ordeal. At 'Hill 60' near Ypres in Belgium the area is now a memorial to what occurred. This is where Todger courageously picked up the fallen standard and carried it forth into battle.

In France, scene of his noblest gallantry, the Somme battlefield still yields up its past. It is estimated that the French Army still disposes annually of 90 tons of armaments that rise to the surface of the fields. More specifically at Morval, scene of Todger's most revered deed of bravery, there is now a quiet rural community of no more than two hundred inhabitants. Back in 1921 the British League of Help asked towns to adopt areas that had been devastated by the conflict, with a view to rebuilding their impoverished war torn surroundings. The city of Canterbury in Kent adopted Morval and the nearby village of Lesboeufs. British aid workers in 1922 found the Morval area to be a bare and treeless environment, littered with shell holes and debris, even though the villagers, who were living in Nissen huts, were working day and night to clear the land.

The people of Canterbury raised £1,174.4s.9d over the coming two years to help plant fruit trees, provide seeds, materials for homes, clothing, re-instate the water supply, and purchase a threshing machine. Time and nature have since performed their own slow healing. Mme D'Hollandler the last elderly villager with childhood memories of Morval during Todger's time, died in the late 1990s. Today there is little to remind of us what happened here but for a small war cemetery on the outskirts of the village, close to where Todger Jones pulled off the deed that was to earn him the Victoria Cross. Morval cemetery records the names of fifty-four British soldiers and a sole German. It is a corner of a foreign field that is forever England, and will always be associated with the humble Cheshire infantryman from Runcorn.

Lest we forget. On Remembrance Day in 2001 the Cheshire regiment still remembers Todger Jones.